EGG
ART

EGG ART

ART

50 Designs to Paint, Dye and Draw

KATYA TRISCHUK

Search Press

Inspiring | Educating | Creating | Entertaining

Brimming with creative inspiration, how-to projects, and useful
information to enrich your everyday life, Quarto Knows is a favourite
destination for those pursuing their interests and passions. Visit our
site and dig deeper with our books into your area of interest:
Quarto Creates, Quarto Cooks, Quarto Homes, Quarto Lives,
Quarto Drives, Quarto Explores, Quarto Gifts, or Quarto Kids.

A QUARTO BOOK

First published in 2019 by
Search Press Ltd
Wellwood
North Farm Road
Tunbridge Wells
Kent TN2 3DR

© 2019 Quarto Publishing PLC
An imprint of The Quarto Group

ISBN 978-1-78221-849-4

10 9 8 7 6 5 4 3 2 1

Conceived, edited and designed by
Quarto Publishing plc,
an imprint of The Quarto Group
6 Blundell Street
London N7 9BH

www.quartoknows.com
QUAR.306955

Senior editor: Kate Burkett
Senior art editor: Emma Clayton
Designer: Eoghan O'Brien
Photographer: Phil Wilkins
Art director: Gemma Wilson
Publisher: Samantha Warrington

MIX
Paper from
responsible sources
FSC® C008047

CONTENTS

MEET KATYA

I never imagined that this would be my job. I always knew I was an artist – I painted and did well on my portfolio projects at university. I am a trained interior designer by profession, but art has shaped my life differently than I planned. I had no idea that I would be doing this for the rest of my life.

I like batik wax-resist art because of the intricacy of the patterns and the surprise reveal of the design once the wax is removed. You don't see the colours side by side, as you do with painting, because wax covers the previous layer. I am a pattern designer at heart. Egg art feels very still and tranquil. I have always worked at a regular size table – nothing too fancy, just a well-lit area. I think that's the reason why this form of visual art has stuck with me over the years; I never needed a huge studio and grand space. I love how basic and simple this art form is, too. I can create egg art with almost nothing – just a carton of eggs and a quick look around the house. You can be creative with eggs in many different ways, and this type of art also doesn't create much waste. It's economical, ecological and very family friendly.

Almost every morning my daughter walks to my studio and asks for an egg to decorate, which got me thinking about how other kids and adults might also enjoy this art craft. For this book, I designed 50 eggs that will appeal to all ages. In my experience, this type of art teaches us to be patient, careful and very creative. I love intertwining rows and rows of ornate lines over the egg, creating complex patterns that I know collectors who are passionate about egg art will love.

Inspiration comes from the colours and shapes of flowers and leaves. Often, I am inspired by fabric or clothing patterns, too, or by the pysanka tradition. A pysanka is a Slavic egg, decorated with traditional folk designs using a wax-resist method. It's impossible to run out of ideas. Each season brings new ideas and inspiration.

You can see more of my egg art on my online shop, Ukrainian Easter Eggs – www.ukrainianeastereggs.store. Through the years I have shipped boxes full of egg art to places as far flung as Australia and Asia, which proves that egg art is an art form suitable for any culture. I hope my readers will find this book both engaging and fun.

TOOLS AND MATERIALS

Egg art is an extremely accessible craft. You can use almost anything and everything to decorate your eggs – from batik egg dyes to food colouring, washi tape to strips of tissue paper, and marker pens to glitter glue. As well as the decorative tools, here is a list of the more practical materials you will need to get creative.

1 EGG BLOWER
A quick and hygienic tool for blowing out an egg.

2 & 3 BATIK EGG DYE
Batik egg dye is an aniline dye specifically used for egg art, which produces extremely intense colours and comes in both powder and liquid form.I use batik egg dye for the majority of my egg art, but you can also use food colouring (24), which is available from all good grocery stores.

5 WHITE VINEGAR
A teaspoon of white vinegar is used to activate the pigment in the batik egg dyes. It is also used for the vinegar-etched projects, whereby the egg is immersed in a jar of vinegar and the calcium in the eggshell breaks down to reveal the shell's underlayer, creating a reversed-out pattern.

6 LONG CANDLE
This is used to heat up and activate the hot-tip stylus pen and then to melt the beeswax off the egg once you have completed the pattern. It can also be used to create simple wax patterns, such as polka dots, on an egg.

7 NEEDLE OR PIN
If you are not using an egg blower, you can use a needle, pin or other pointed-end tool to make a hole in the bottom and top of the egg from which you can blow out the contents.

9 CRAFT KNIFE
A craft knife is handy for correcting any mistakes made with a hot-tip stylus pen and beeswax. Use it to gently scrape off the beeswax where it is not needed.

13 PENCIL
When you first start practising egg art, it is a good idea to draw your pattern on the egg in pencil first before going over the lines with beeswax. In the projects, I have drawn directly onto the egg with my stylus and beeswax, but I recommend beginners draw the pattern with a pencil first, as is described in the step-by-steps.

14 EGG
The majority of projects in this book require a chicken egg; however, you can use a duck or even an ostrich egg.

17, 18 & 19 BEESWAX STRIPS, SHEETS AND BLOCKS
Beeswax is used to seal the colour of the egg, protecting the covered areas from the dye that is being applied and producing a decorative pattern. It is available in strips, sheets and blocks as well as a variety of colours; I mainly stick to black. For more complex patterns and projects that require multiple dyeing stages, I recommend using two or more colours to make it easier to keep track of where you are.

20 & 21 HOT-TIP STYLUS PENS
Throughout the book, I use small, medium and large stylus pens. Use the small stylus for fine, delicate lines; a large stylus for filling in large sections; and a medium stylus for everything else.

22 SMALL TOOTHBRUSH
Used to remove the outer layer of eggshell on an egg that has been submerged in vinegar.

23 PAINT
Feel free to use any type of paint medium, including acrylic and watercolour paints.

24 FOOD COLOURING
Available from all good grocery shops, food colouring is ideal for making kid-friendly, edible egg art.

OTHER MATERIALS
Tealight (4)
Teaspoon (8)
Lighter (10)
Metallic markers (11)
Fine-tipped marker pen (12)
Glitter glue (15)
Paintbrushes (16)

NOT PICTURED
Jars
Latex gloves
Paper towels
Tissues

1/ EGG ART PROJECTS

COLOUR BLOCK EGG

Colour Blocking with Dye

This is an easy, worry-free project, and even an egg that goes wrong ends up looking great. These eggs look fantastic displayed in a group, perhaps in a glass bowl. I used pastel baby nursery colours, which means they could be turned into a baby mobile for little eyes to explore the colours and shapes. You can also make edible versions of this egg using hardboiled white eggs and a food-colouring kit.

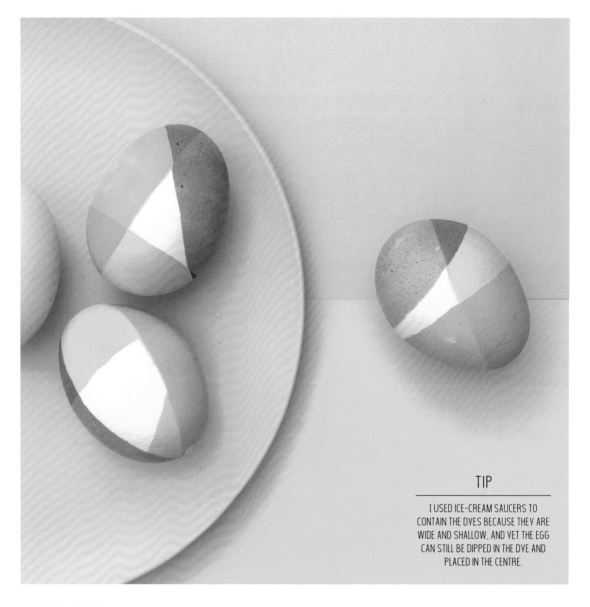

TIP

I USED ICE-CREAM SAUCERS TO
CONTAIN THE DYES BECAUSE THEY ARE
WIDE AND SHALLOW, AND YET THE EGG
CAN STILL BE DIPPED IN THE DYE AND
PLACED IN THE CENTRE.

YOU WILL NEED

- Three hollow white chicken eggs
- Candle
- Lighter or matches
- Beeswax

- Hot-tip stylus pen (medium size)
- Three eggshell dyes in yellow, green and blue
- Three shallow containers

- Three teaspoons of white vinegar
- Three teaspoons
- Tissues

1 Close up the holes in the bottom of the eggs with beeswax (see page 124). Fill a container with the first dye, in this case yellow (don't use a lot of dye or the eggs will float too much). Dip about half of the first egg in the dye and hold it down for a few minutes until you see that the dye has taken. Let dry.

2 Dip the egg in a container filled with the green dye, holding it at a different angle, then let dry.

3 Go on to the next colour, dipping the egg in a container filled with blue dye. Try to create interesting colour-block shapes. Let dry as before.

4 Take another egg and repeat the process, dipping it in the yellow dye first, but this time at a different angle.

5 Again, dip the second egg in the green dye, varying the angle.

6 Dip the second egg in the blue dye, remembering to alter the angle so that the dyed eggs look different. Repeat the process for the third egg (or for as many eggs as you want to dip and dye).

PEACOCK FEATHERS EGG

Four-colour Dye and Gold Paint

This egg would make a trendy keepsake and table décor for a wedding. The design for this egg has a strong spiritual meaning for people from cultures in which the peacock is worshipped. In wedding décor, for example, a peacock theme represents wealth and prosperity. It is a beautiful and thoughtful keepsake and gift idea.

TIP

YOU CAN USE A GOLD MARKER PEN OR
NAIL VARNISH TO ADD THE GOLD
DETAILING, BUT ACRYLIC PAINT IS BEST
BECAUSE IT DRIES QUICKLY.

- One hollow white chicken egg
- Candle
- Lighter or matches
- Hot-tip stylus pen (medium size)
- Beeswax

- Four eggshell dyes in blue, green, purple and black
- Four containers with lids
- Four teaspoons of white vinegar
- Four teaspoons

- Paper towels
- Tissues
- Gold acrylic paint
- Fine craft paintbrush

1 Close up the hole in the bottom of the egg with beeswax (see page 124). Submerge the egg in the blue dye for 10 minutes or so, then remove and blot dry with a paper towel. Working from the bottom of the egg to the top, draw four or five peacock feathers around the egg, adding an eye-like shape at the top of each one. Make some of the feathers shorter and some longer. Let dry.

2 Submerge the egg in the green dye for 10 minutes or so, then remove and blot dry with a clean paper towel.

3 To preserve the green colour, fill the main part inside each peacock 'eye' with beeswax. Let dry.

4 Submerge the egg in the purple dye for 10 minutes or so, then remove and blot dry with a clean paper towel. Before submerging the egg in the next dye, fill in around the perimeter and inside of all the eyes with beeswax. Let dry.

5 Submerge the egg in the black dye for 10 minutes or so, then remove and blot dry with a clean paper towel. Hold the egg close to the candle flame and start removing the melting wax with a tissue (see page 125). Keep turning the egg, holding it near the flame, gently cleaning off the wax.

6 Using the paintbrush, add light brushstrokes of gold acrylic paint over and around the feathers. You need to build up the gold paint in stages, so start with a small amount and let dry before adding more strokes. Allow to dry completely.

WHITE POLKA-DOT EGG

Drop and Dye Dots

Batik is an age-old decorating technique in which the artist uses beeswax to prevent dye penetrating cloth or, in this case, the surface of an egg. When the wax is removed, the original base colour is revealed. Here the technique is used to create a striking polka-dot design.

- One hollow white chicken egg
- Candle
- Lighter or matches
- Hot-tip stylus pen (medium size)
- Beeswax

- Thin beeswax candle (as you would use for a birthday cake)
- Craft knife
- Blue eggshell dye
- Container with a lid

- One teaspoon of white vinegar
- Teaspoon
- Paper towels
- Tissues

1 Close up the hole in the bottom of the egg with beeswax (see page 124). Light the thin candle, point it downwards and start dripping little drops of wax onto one side of the egg. You can stop the wax dripping by holding the candle upright again.

2 Continue dripping more drops of wax onto the same side of the egg, making sure they are evenly sized and spaced, then let dry.

3 Slowly turn the egg and keep adding more drops of wax, letting each area dry before going on to the next. If the candle drips too fast, turn it upright again to control the flow of wax.

4 If you make a mistake, use a craft knife to scrape the wax off gently.

5 Submerge the egg in the blue dye for 10 minutes or so, then remove and blot dry with a paper towel.

6 Use the large candle to remove the drops of wax. Hold the egg close to the candle flame and start removing the melting wax with a tissue (see page 125). Keep turning the egg, holding it near the flame and gently cleaning off the wax.

BOHEMIAN FLORAL EGG

Five-colour Dye with Pysanky Colours

Inspired by traditional pysanky folk art embellishments on clothing, scarves, embroidered shawls and coats, the stylized flowers on this egg look fantastical and aren't found in nature. This is one of my oldest designs and a favourite with customers all year around. The dye colours used for this egg are very traditional – I refer to them as the traditional pysanky dye set.

- One hollow white chicken egg
- Candle
- Lighter or matches
- Hot-tip stylus pens (small and medium size)

- Beeswax
- Pencil
- Five eggshell dyes in yellow, green, orange, red and black
- Five containers with lids

- Five teaspoons of white vinegar
- Five teaspoons
- Paper towels
- Tissues

1 Close up the hole in the bottom of the egg with beeswax (see page 124). Submerge the egg in the yellow dye for 10 minutes or so, then remove and blot dry with a paper towel. Use a pencil to draw the first of four flowers on the egg. Add three more flowers, alternating them so you have two flowers higher up and two lower down. Add some leaves, too. Using the small stylus pen go over your linework with beeswax (see page 123) and let dry.

2 Submerge the egg in the green dye for 10 minutes or so, then remove and blot dry with a clean paper towel. Use beeswax and the medium stylus pen to fill in the leaves and centres of the flowers. Add a row of dots (i.e. the stamens) above each flower; these elements will stay green when the egg is dipped in the next dye.

3 Submerge the egg in the orange dye for 10 minutes or so, then remove and blot dry with a clean paper towel. Fill in the central petal supporting the stamens in each flower.

4 Submerge the egg in the red dye for 10 minutes or so, remove and blot dry with a clean paper towel. Fill in the petals of the flowers with beeswax.

5 Submerge the egg in the black dye for 10 minutes or so, remove and blot dry. To reveal the fantastic colours, hold the egg close to the candle flame and start removing the melting wax with a tissue (see page 125). Keep turning the egg, holding it near the flame, gently cleaning off the wax.

JAPANESE FAN EGG

Repeating Half-moon Pattern

Japanese fans are very ornate, with a pattern that resembles the scales of koi carp. This pattern has a great symbolism, acting like a shield that covers and protects. Indeed, many tattoo artists use scale motifs in their body-art designs. I have also seen this pattern in upholstery fabrics and even marble tiles. These eggs would make the perfect housewarming gift, acting as a symbol of protection and strength for a new home.

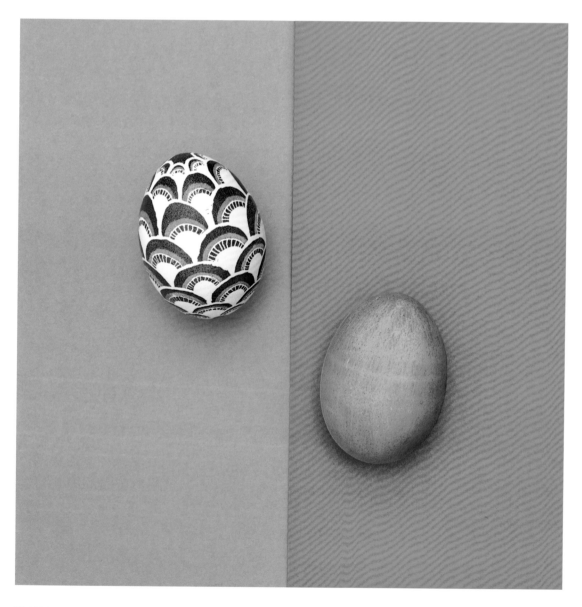

- One hollow white chicken egg
- Candle
- Lighter or matches
- Hot-tip stylus pens (small and medium size)

- Beeswax (in two different colours)
- Pencil
- Two eggshell dyes in red and blue
- Two containers with lids
- Two teaspoons of white vinegar

- Two teaspoons
- Paper towels
- Tissue paper

1 Close up the hole in the bottom of the egg (see page 124). In pencil, draw six petals around the beeswax seal to create a daisy. Join the tips of the petals with a curved line to create a row of half-moons. Using the small stylus pen, go over your linework with the first beeswax colour (see page 123), then let dry.

2 Working from the bottom to the top of the egg, use the medium stylus pen and beeswax to draw another row of half-moons and start creating a series of fan shapes. Fill in the middle of each fan shape with beeswax, so that it will stay white after dyeing.

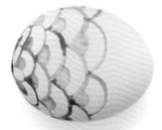

3 Continue drawing and filling in more fan shapes, making them larger as you reach the middle of the egg and smaller as you move towards the top.

4 To add extra detail, use the small stylus pen to add a thin lined border around the filled-in area of each fan shape.

5 Submerge the egg in the red dye for 10 minutes or so, remove, and blot dry with a paper towel. Then, using the medium stylus pen, draw a thick border in the second beeswax colour around the filled-in areas inside each fan shape.

6 Blue is your last colour. Submerge the egg in the blue dye for 10 minutes or so, remove and blot dry with a clean paper towel. To finish, hold the egg close to the candle flame and start removing the melting wax with a tissue (see page 125). Keep turning the egg, holding it near the flame, gently cleaning off the wax.

THE HUNTER BULL'S-EYE AND ARROW EGG

Archery Motifs

Taking inspiration from early man's drawings on stones and Viking arrows, a simple egg such as this makes a great gift and home décor accessory for friends and relatives. It would also be the perfect gift for someone who enjoys archery.

- One hollow white chicken egg
- Candle
- Lighter or matches
- Hot-tip stylus pens (small and medium size)

- Beeswax
- Pencil
- Black eggshell dye
- Container with lid
- One teaspoon of white vinegar

- Teaspoon
- Paper towels
- Tissues

1 Close up the hole in the bottom of the egg (see page 124). Using the medium stylus pen, divide the egg into eight equal sections by drawing a line from top to bottom on both sides of the egg, then drawing a line around the middle. Draw diagonal pencil lines, on both sides of the egg, to establish the outline of the two bull's-eye motifs. Use the small stylus pen to join the ends of these lines to create the outer circle of the bull's-eyes.

2 Working from the centre, add a dot of beeswax and draw in more circles for the two bull's-eye motifs, spacing them as evenly as possible. Go over your linework with beeswax (see page 123) and let dry.

3 Using the stylus pen and beeswax, add feathered arrows to the dividing lines on both sides of the egg, pointing towards the bull's-eye motifs.

4 Fill alternate rings in the bull's-eye motifs with short, evenly spaced lines. Turn the egg and draw two smaller arrows, which cross each other, in the empty spaces around the bull's-eye motifs.

5 To make the pattern more ornate, add some larger dots of beeswax and some smaller dots surrounded by lined rings along the two vertical dividing lines, as shown.

6 Once the egg is filled with decorative elements and there are no empty spaces, it's ready for dyeing. Submerge the egg in the black dye for 10 minutes or so, then remove and blot dry with a paper towel. To finish, hold the egg close to the candle flame and start removing the melting wax with a tissue (see page 125).

COLOURFUL PEBBLES EGG

Beeswax and Four-Colour Dye

For this organic design, take inspiration from the world around you, studying loose rocks and pebbles, the flat stones of the surfaces in passages and walkways, and naturally shaped stone slabs or rock tiles in your garden. The dyes for this egg should range in tone from lighter to darker. I chose yellow, orange, red and dark red.

YOU WILL NEED

- One hollow white chicken egg
- Candle
- Lighter or matches
- Hot-tip stylus pens (small and medium size)

- Beeswax (in two or three different colours)
- Pencil
- Four eggshell dyes in orange, yellow, red and dark red
- Four containers with lids

- Four teaspoons of white vinegar
- Four teaspoons
- Paper towels
- Tissues

1 Close up the hole in the bottom of the egg with beeswax (see page 124). Map out the shape of the pebbles all over the egg in pencil, keeping most of them medium sized but adding some slightly smaller and larger ones here and there. You are aiming for a series of regular organic shapes. Using the small stylus pen, outline all the pebble shapes with small dots of beeswax and let dry.

2 Submerge the egg in the orange dye for 10 minutes or so, remove and blot dry with a paper towel.

3 Using the medium stylus pen, draw another pebble inside each of the shapes, as shown. It can be helpful to use beeswax in a different colour.

4 Submerge the egg in the yellow dye for 10 minutes or so, then remove and blot dry with a clean paper towel. Again, draw another pebble in beeswax inside each of the shapes.

5 Submerge the egg in the red dye for 10 minutes or so, then remove and blot dry with a clean paper towel. Fill each of the shapes completely with beeswax.

6 Dark red is the last colour. Submerge the egg in the dark red dye for 10 minutes or so, then remove and blot dry, as before. To finish, hold the egg close to the candle flame and start removing the melting wax with a tissue (see page 125). Keep turning the egg, holding it near the flame, gently cleaning off the wax.

BABY GIRL KEEPSAKE EGG

Single-colour Dye with Crosshatching Effect

This batik egg makes a beautiful and meaningful gift that you can customize – perhaps with a birthday or baptism date, or a new baby's name. Just find a spot to write somewhere on the egg and this will become a very thoughtful gift. The design includes symbols of nets to 'catch' good luck.

TIP
_____

TO MAKE A KEEPSAKE FOR A BABY
BOY, USE A BLUE EGGSHELL DYE
INSTEAD OF PINK – OR USE ANY
COLOUR YOU PREFER!

- One hollow white chicken egg
- Candle
- Lighter or matches
- Hot-tip stylus pens (small and large size)
- Beeswax

- Pencil
- Pink eggshell dye
- One container with lid
- One teaspoon of white vinegar
- Teaspoon

- Paper towels
- Tissues

1 Close up the hole in the bottom of the egg with beeswax (see page 124). Using a pencil and working from top to bottom, draw a 'belt' with a thin border along both edges all around the egg. Add a row of diamond shapes to the belt. Draw a stylized cross with swirls at the ends on both sides of the egg.

2 Using the small stylus pen, go over your linework with beeswax (see page 123) and let dry. Using the same stylus pen, draw four petals with a narrow border around each cross and fill the crosses with crosshatched lines. Leave an empty square where the arms of the crosses overlap.

3 Turn the egg on its side and fill the diamonds in the belt with more crosshatched lines.

4 Add a series of equally spaced dots above and below the belt, and small dashes between the diamonds inside. Fill the centre of both crosses with beeswax, but leave a square of white space and add a small dot inside. Switch to the large stylus pen and fill in the petals around the crosses with solid beeswax. Let dry.

5 Submerge the egg in the pink dye for 10 minutes or so, then remove and blot dry with a paper towel.

6 Hold the egg close to the candle flame and start removing the melting wax with a tissue (see page 125). Keep turning the egg, holding it near the flame, gently cleaning off the wax.

DECORATIVE BELTS EGG

Dotted Crosses and Organic Shapes

This colourful egg combines stylized crosses with organic shapes. Although the design looks complicated, it is actually quite easy to create. Easter-time décor and gift ideas for family and friends are the inspiration here. You could display a group of these eggs in a church basket for Easter, perhaps next to some festive Paska bread, which is made with lots of eggs and raisins and is traditionally eaten at Easter in the Ukraine.

TIP

USING A MEDIUM STYLUS PEN SPEEDS
UP THE MARKING PROCESS WHEN YOU
HAVE LARGE AREAS TO FILL WITH
BEESWAX.

- One hollow white chicken egg
- Candle
- Lighter or matches
- Hot-tip stylus pens (small and medium size)

- Beeswax
- Pencil
- Three eggshell dyes in yellow, green and red
- Three containers with lids

- Three teaspoons of white vinegar
- Three teaspoons
- Paper towels
- Tissues

1 Close up the hole in the bottom of the egg (see page 124). Using a pencil, divide the egg into four equal sections, from top to bottom, by drawing parallel lines to create two 'belts' around the egg. Draw another belt around the middle of the egg. You should now have eight equal-sized triangles, four on one side of the egg and four on the other. Using the small stylus pen go over your linework with beeswax (see page 123) and let dry.

2 Use the medium stylus pen to add large dots of beeswax to the belts running around the egg and to fill in the squares where the belts cross. Let the beeswax dry, then submerge the egg in the yellow dye for 10 minutes or so, remove and blot dry with a paper towel.

3 Using the medium stylus pen again, add a large dot of beeswax to the middle of each triangle. Then use the small stylus pen to draw three lines from the central dot to the corners of each triangle. Draw two swirls, one pointing left and one right, on either side of the three lines in each triangle. Let the beeswax dry.

4 Submerge the egg in the green dye for 10 minutes or so, then remove and blot dry with a clean paper towel. Fill the three belts with beeswax to preserve the green colour underneath and let dry.

5 Your last colour is red. Submerge the egg in the red dye for 10 minutes or so – enough time for it to overpower the green dye. As before, remove the egg from the dye and blot dry with a clean paper towel.

6 To finish, hold the egg close to the candle flame and start removing the melting wax with a tissue (see page 125). Keep turning the egg, holding it near the flame, gently cleaning off the wax.

YELLOW GEOMETRY EGG

Striped Geometric Triangles

The design of this egg, with its regular pattern and textural feel, makes it ideal for adding visual interest to a simple home décor. These eggs are very modern – perfect for a Swedish interior design in which the blue and yellow act as accents in a stark white room. Less is definitely more here. I suggest placing a few of these eggs with others dyed in solid blue and yellow.

TIP

FOR THIS EGG, MANY AREAS NEED
FILLING IN WITH SOLID COLOUR, SO I
SUGGEST USING A LARGER STYLUS
PEN WITH A GREATER FLOW. A PEN
WITH A LARGE FLOW GIVES A BOLDER
PATTERN, WHILE A FINER PEN WILL
TAKE LONGER BUT ALLOW YOU TO ADD
MORE TRIANGLES TO THE DESIGN. HERE,
I USED A MEDIUM-SIZE STYLUS PEN.

- One hollow chicken egg
- Candle
- Lighter or matches
- Hot-tip stylus pens (small and medium size)

- Beeswax
- Pencil
- Two eggshell dyes in yellow and blue
- Two containers with lids
- Two teaspoons of white vinegar

- Two teaspoons
- Paper towels
- Tissues

1 Close up the hole in the bottom of the egg (see page 124), then submerge in the yellow dye for 10 minutes, remove and blot dry with a paper towel. Using a pencil, divide the egg into eight equal vertical sections and four equal horizontal sections.

2 Once the egg is divided into sections, go over your linework with beeswax and the small stylus pen (see page 123). Let dry.

3 Use the small stylus pen and beeswax to draw diagonal lines in each section, making sure that they all point in the same direction.

4 Half-fill each section with beeswax, then add a parallel line and a row of evenly spaced lines along the base of each filled-in triangle. Fill in the star shape at the top of the egg with beeswax, so that it will stay yellow in the final design.

5 Submerge the egg in the blue dye for 10 minutes or so, then remove and blot dry with a paper towel.

6 To finish, hold the egg close to the candle flame and start removing the melting wax with a tissue (see page 125). Keep turning the egg, holding it near the flame, gently cleaning off the wax.

RED-AND-WHITE CANDY CANE EGG

Calligraphic Pattern

Red and white creates a classic colour combination recalling festive Christmas décor, shop windows in winter, sweet wrappers, and gift boxes. These eggs, with their ornate, calligraphic design, make a great gift for family and friends.

TIP

IN STEP 3, DRAWING ONLY FIVE LINES
AND DIVIDING THE EGG INTO SIX
SECTIONS WILL PRODUCE AN EGG WITH
A LARGER, BOLDER PATTERN.

- One hollow white chicken egg
- Candle
- Lighter or matches
- Hot-tip stylus pen (medium size)
- Beeswax

- Pencil
- Red eggshell dye
- Container with lid
- One teaspoon of white vinegar
- Teaspoon

- Paper towels
- Tissues

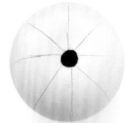

1 Close up the hole in the bottom of the egg with beeswax (see page 124). Using a pencil, divide the egg into four sections from top to bottom. Divide each of these sections into two to create a total of eight sections.

2 Turn the egg on its side and draw a line around the middle. Draw another line on either side of this central line to create four sections that run around the egg.

3 Divide each of the four sections in half, so that you have seven lines creating eight even sections for filling in with stylized S-shapes. Working on one side of the egg at a time, draw the outline of the S-shapes in pencil, then outline and fill them in with beeswax using the stylus pen. Make sure the S-shapes point in the opposite direction where they touch in each section.

4 Turn the egg and continue drawing and filling in the S-shapes in the other sections until the egg is completely covered with the design. Let the beeswax dry before turning the egg and filling in more sections. The pencil-drawn grid should help you maintain a regular pattern of S-shapes.

5 Submerge the egg in the red dye for 10 minutes or so. Remove the egg from the dye and blot dry with a paper towel.

6 To finish, hold the egg close to the candle flame and start removing the melting wax with a tissue (see page 125). Keep turning the egg, holding it near the flame, and gently cleaning off the wax.

BLUE STARBURST EGG

Three-colour Dye and Starburst

I have many designs that are people's favourites and many are bestsellers, but this blue egg is the most popular. Sometimes I make three of these in one day and ship them to different parts of the world. I don't know why people like this egg so much. I think the starburst or mandala is very appealing. I am showing a simplified version here. It has the same colour combination and design as the one I make for clients, but is less complicated.

TIP

THE COLOUR OF THE BEESWAX IN STEP 1 IS IMPORTANT. I USED RED BEESWAX TO CONTRAST WITH THE BLUE DYES. IF YOU USE BLUE BEESWAX AND THEN DYE IN BLUE, YOU WILL BE WORKING IN THE DARK.

- One hollow white chicken egg
- Candle
- Lighter or matches
- Hot-tip stylus pens (small and medium size)

- Beeswax
- Pencil (optional)
- Three eggshell dyes in turquoise, blue and black
- Three containers with lids

- Three teaspoons of white vinegar
- Three teaspoons
- Paper towels
- Tissues
- Craft knife (optional)

1 Close up the hole in the bottom of the egg with beeswax (see page 124). Using the small stylus pen and red beeswax, draw two parallel 'belts' with narrow borders from the bottom of the egg to the top. Add a row of diamond shapes to the narrow space between the belts and a row of triangles along the inside edge of each belt. Add an eight-pointed star to the centre of both sides of the egg. Let dry.

2 Add a dot to the centre of both stars, then, following the pattern in the photograph, add rows of thick dashes, dots, chevrons and smaller eight-pointed stars where shown.

3 Continue adding details to the white areas, embellishing the eight-pointed stars with inner petals and adding a fringed crosshatch surround.

4 Submerge the egg in the turquoise dye for 10 minutes or so, then remove and blot dry with a paper towel. Use the black beeswax to add more rows of dots, outline the two large, eight-pointed stars, and surround the other stars with square borders, as indicated in the photograph. Let dry.

5 Submerge the egg in the blue dye for 10 minutes or so, then remove and blot dry with a clean paper towel. Using the medium stylus pen and black beeswax, fill in the belts and add a border to the tiny triangles edging the inside of the belts. Finally, fill the triangles with a crosshatched pattern. These areas are to remain blue.

6 Submerge the egg in the black dye for 10 minutes or so, then remove and blot dry with a clean paper towel. Hold the egg close to the candle flame and start removing the melting wax with a tissue (see page 125). Keep turning the egg, holding it near the flame, gently cleaning off the wax.

NEOLITHIC POTTERY EGG

Primitive Drawing

My inspiration for this egg comes from many places, including monthly trips to the anthropological/ancient history section of my local museum. Primitive drawings from Neolithic times show goddesses, fish and mammals, snakes, watchful eyes and water – all motifs that are common in many parts of the world. I selected snakes, watchful eyes and fish for this egg, which basically represents a full belly and a safe home. This protective egg brings good fortune.

TIP

EGGS THAT ARE A LIGHTER SHADE OF BROWN WILL TAKE BOTH ORANGE AND RED DYES WELL. THE COLOUR WON'T BE AS VIVID AS ON A WHITE EGG, BUT IT WILL GIVE THE EGG A RUSTIC, TERRACOTTA POTTERY LOOK.

- One hollow brown chicken egg
- Candle
- Lighter or matches
- Hot-tip stylus pen (medium size)
- Beeswax

- Pencil
- Black eggshell dye
- Container with lid
- One teaspoon of white vinegar
- Teaspoon

- Paper towels
- Tissues

1 Close up the hole in the bottom of the egg with beeswax (see page 124). Using a pencil, draw two 'belts' composed of four closely spaced lines at the top and bottom. To create the 'eye' pattern, draw a series of evenly spaced, wave-like shapes above the bottom belt. Go over your linework with beeswax (see page 123) and let dry.

2 Turn the egg and add another series of 'waves' in beeswax, this time coming from the top belt and facing in the opposite direction. Let dry.

3 Connect the waves where they 'overlap' to create a circle for the eyes and add a dot to the centre for the pupils. Fill the spaces in between the belts and waves with evenly spaced lines.

4 Add a series of snake-like shapes in the spaces between the waves. Draw a thicker line above the top and bottom belts and add a row of dot-filled circles above these lines. Be sure to leave enough space above the top and bottom belts for the fish design.

5 Draw a couple of primitive fish at the top and bottom of the egg. If you find a fish too difficult, draw a sun or the yin-yang symbol instead.

6 Submerge the egg in the black dye for 10 minutes or so, then remove and blot dry with a paper towel. To reveal the design, hold the egg close to the candle flame and start removing the melting wax with a tissue (see page 125). Keep turning the egg, holding it near the flame, and gently cleaning off the wax.

ZIGZAG HIPSTER EGG

Single-colour Dye with Zigzag Pattern

I designed this funky-looking egg when chevron fabric was super trendy, which is why 'hipster' is part of the name. You can use a single dye colour or two colours. I've kept this egg simple, but played around with scale and size, as well as the length of the dyeing process, which affects the intensity of the colour.

- One hollow white chicken egg
- Candle
- Lighter or matches
- Hot-tip stylus pen (large size)
- Beeswax

- Pencil
- Green eggshell dye
- Container with lid
- One teaspoon of white vinegar
- Teaspoon

- Paper towels
- Tissues

1 Close up the hole in the bottom of the egg with beeswax (see page 124). Using a pencil, divide the egg into eight equal sections from top to bottom. These sections will be filled with lines to create the zigzag pattern. Use the pencil to draw four zigzagging lines in the first two sections. Try to establish the angle and spacing of the lines – these first lines will affect the success of the remaining ones. Go over your linework with beeswax (see page 123) and let dry.

2 Continue adding more lines to the first two sections.

3 Keep adding more lines as you work around the egg, ensuring that the lines in adjoining sections go in opposite directions in order to create the zigzag effect.

4 Continue in this way until all eight sections are filled with evenly spaced lines.

5 Submerge the egg in the green dye for 10 minutes or so, then remove and blot dry with a paper towel.

6 Hold the egg close to the candle flame and start removing the melting wax with a tissue (see page 125). Keep turning the egg, holding it near the flame, gently cleaning off the wax.

DAMASK MEDALLION EGG

Black Filigree Pattern

Reminiscent of the wallpaper found in lavish boutiques and elegant hotels, the design for this egg is based on organic patterns with floral elements. Decorating this egg gives you an opportunity to test your creativity. The egg looks great in black-brown mixes as well as black and white. Try making a few solid black eggs and displaying them with a black-and-white one. In this project, use a larger stylus pen, as the lines need to be thick for the medallion to stand out.

YOU WILL NEED

- One hollow white chicken egg
- Candle
- Lighter or matches
- Hot-tip stylus pens (small and medium size)

- Beeswax
- Pencil
- Black eggshell dye
- Container with lid
- One teaspoon of white vinegar

- Teaspoon
- Paper towels
- Tissues

1 Close up the hole in the bottom of the egg (see page 124). Using a pencil, divide the egg into four equal sections on both sides. Using a medium stylus pen, draw a teardrop in the centre on one side of the egg.

2 Embellish the teardrop by adding a leaf shape with a lined border and four dots down the middle.

3 Give the teardrop a stronger outline and add four swirls that twist left and right at the top and bottom of the egg. Repeat this design on the other side of the egg to produce a symmetrical pattern.

4 Working outwards, use a small stylus pen to add more lines, dots, scalloped edges, swirls and plumes. Make some of these elements more pronounced.

5 Turn the egg and fill in the empty spaces between the two medallions with more swirls, dots, and short lines. Go over your linework with beeswax (see page 123), then let dry.

6 Submerge the egg in the black dye for 10 minutes or so, then remove and blot dry with a paper towel. To finish, hold the egg close to the candle flame and start removing the melting wax with a tissue (see page 125). Keep turning the egg, holding it near the flame, gently cleaning off the wax.

FORTY-EIGHT TRIANGLES EGG

Beeswax and One-colour Dye

This is traditional Pysanka egg pattern, dating back centuries. It may look challenging, but it's worth it once you see the finished result. Once the egg has been successfully divided into 48 triangles, the design possibilities are endless.

- One hollow white chicken egg
- Candle
- Lighter or matches
- Hot-tip stylus pen (medium size)
- Beeswax

- Pencil
- Burgundy eggshell dye
- Container with lid
- One teaspoon of white vinegar
- Teaspoon

- Paper towels
- Tissues

1 Close up the hole in the bottom of the egg with beeswax (see page 124). Using a pencil, divide the egg into four sections from top to bottom. Divide each of these four sections into two, to create eight, and then draw a horizontal line around the middle of the egg.

2 Draw two lines from the middle line toward the top of the egg – one going around the front of the egg in a semi-circular shape, the other going around the back in a semi-circular shape. Connect the lines on the opposite side of the egg to create an oval shape on top of the egg.

3 Staying in the top half of the egg, draw a semi-circle on the side of the egg. Repeat on the other side.

4 Repeat steps 2 and 3 on the bottom half of the egg.

5 Fill in one triangle with thin lines and one with a single large dot, then alternate, ensuring no two triangles next to each other contain the same design.

6 Go over your linework with beeswax (see page 123), let dry, then submerge the egg in the burgundy dye. After 10 minutes or so, remove the egg and blot dry with a paper towel. Hold the egg close to a candle flame and start removing the melting wax with a tissue (see page 125). Keep turning the egg, holding it near the flame, gently cleaning off the wax.

GLITTERY ORANGE ABSTRACT EGG

Taped Shapes and Glitter

This is a fun and colourful egg, and you don't need too many art materials. You can use any type of tape, although I like to use masking tape. You'll also need some gold glitter, perhaps from a children's craft kit. A collection of these modern eggs would look great in a contemporary home setting, especially in a colourful plastic bowl or tray.

- One hollow white chicken egg
- Candle
- Lighter or matches
- Hot-tip stylus pen (medium size)
- Beeswax

- Masking tape
- Scissors
- Orange eggshell dye
- Container with lid
- One teaspoon of white vinegar

- Teaspoon
- Paper towels
- Tissues
- Gold glitter

1 Close up the hole in the bottom of the egg with beeswax (see page 124). Cut small triangles from the masking tape, one at a time, and press them onto the egg, altering the direction of each to create an interesting pattern.

2 Continue cutting out and sticking on triangles until the egg is covered. Make sure the triangles are evenly spaced – some can sit closer together or even overlap.

3 Submerge the egg in the orange dye for 10 minutes or so, then remove and blot dry with a paper towel.

4 Start carefully peeling the pieces of tape from the egg.

5 Remove the rest of the pieces of tape. Don't worry about the sticky residue left behind, as these areas will be covered with glitter.

6 Take a tissue and open it out. Place the egg in the centre of the tissue and sprinkle over some glitter. Roll the egg in the glitter until it is nicely covered. Check whether there are any sticky areas remaining and sprinkle over more glitter if necessary.

FISH SCALES EGG

Beeswax and One-colour Dye

Bring the outside in with this egg art design! Inspired by patterns in nature, this egg resembles a pine cone. The colour blue brings beachy, seaside vibes to the home and is the perfect adornment for your summer table set-up.

- One hollow white chicken egg
- Candle
- Lighter or matches
- Hot-tip stylus pen (medium size)
- Beeswax

- Pencil
- Turquoise eggshell dye
- Container with lid
- One teaspoon of white vinegar
- Teaspoon

- Paper towels
- Tissues

1 Close up the hole at the bottom of the egg with beeswax (see page 124). Using a pencil, draw eight petals around the hole.

2 Draw semi-circles from one petal to the next to create a row of half-moons.

3 Continue adding rows of half-moons, making each row bigger than the last as you move towards the middle of the egg. Fill in the space between the eight petals you drew in step 1.

4 Start to fill in the middle of each half-moon.

5 Once you reach the middle of the egg, start to reduce the size of the half-moons as you move towards the top of the egg. Leave the top of the egg clear and fill in the middle of the rest of the half-moons.

6 Go over your linework with beeswax (see page 123), let dry, then submerge the egg in the turquoise dye. After 10 minutes or so, remove and blot dry with a paper towel. Hold the egg close to the candle flame and start removing the melting wax with a tissue (see page 125). Keep turning the egg, holding it near the flame, gently cleaning off the wax.

GENDER-REVEAL GOLD CRACKABLE EGG

Single-colour Paint and Egg Filling

This is a fun idea for delivering breaking news, such as the gender of a baby, an engagement announcement, news of an adoption or anything special you want to tell your family and friends. Simply insert strips of coloured tissue paper or ribbon, or perhaps some confetti, into these golden eggs and surprise your guests at a party. Nobody will suspect that the eggs in the centre of the white are messengers delivering exciting news.

YOU WILL NEED

- One hollow brown chicken egg
- Gold acrylic paint
- Craft paintbrush
- Pink or blue tissue paper or raffia or ribbon
- Scissors

1 Ensure that the hole in the egg is slightly larger than usual and wash the egg well. Holding the egg at the top and bottom, use a small amount of gold acrylic paint to paint one side with loose brushstrokes. Apply the paint lightly so that it dries fast.

2 Turn the egg and continue applying paint until the other side is covered. Let dry.

3 Once the egg is painted on both sides, paint the top and bottom. Let dry and apply another coat of paint all over to ensure good coverage.

4 Cut the tissue paper, raffia or ribbon into thin strips. Carefully insert the strips into the egg and tuck any ends away in order to conceal the surprise.

TIP

IF YOU ARE USING CONFETTI OR SOMETHING SIMILAR, WHICH MAY FALL OUT OF THE EGG, USE A TINY BLOB OF BEESWAX TO SEAL THE HOLE AND THEN PAINT OVER IT WITH GOLD ACRYLIC PAINT.

INDIAN TREASURE EGG

Henna Pattern with Beeswax

My daughter Maya came home one day with her hands painted with henna. She'd had a fun activity day with her Indian teacher celebrating Indian heritage. The kids snacked on samosas and had their hands painted. I made a note to create a golden egg embossed with red beeswax to look like henna. You can use black beeswax instead of red.

- One hollow brown chicken egg
- Gold acrylic paint　　　·
- Craft paintbrush
- Candle
- Lighter or matches

- Hot-tip stylus pen (medium size)
- Beeswax

1 Hold the egg at the top and bottom, and paint one side with gold acrylic paint. Keep turning and painting the egg until both sides are solid gold. Let dry, then apply more paint to the top and bottom of the egg. Using a medium stylus pen to give a nice flow of wax, draw a flower in beeswax around the hole at the bottom of the egg and let dry.

2 Working from the bottom to the top of the egg, apply more beeswax to create an organic Paisley pattern of swirls and dots. Imagine you are recreating the pattern of an Indian sari.

3 Keep working up from the bottom, expanding the design and adding a floral fan on one side of the egg.

4 Add more decorations, such as a branch of leaves edged with dots. Ensure the egg is covered evenly with organic patterns, and let dry.

TIP

TRY ADDING AN ATTACHMENT AND TURNING THE EGG INTO A NAMED ORNAMENT. OR MAKE A FEW PATTERNED EGGS AND DISPLAY THEM WITH SOME SOLID GOLD ONES FOR A NICE TABLE CENTREPIECE.

WINTER STAR EGG

Snowflakes in Blue and White

The inspiration behind this design is winter, snowflakes, crisp, cold air and frozen rivers. A collection of these eggs would look great hanging as ornaments on a tree. They can also be made into personalized gifts – you could use the stylus pen to add the recipient's name and perhaps the date on the bottom of the egg. If you are turning the egg into a hanging ornament, try suspending it with some silver twine or an old silver necklace chain.

TIP

IF THE SECOND BLUE DYE DOES NOT TAKE VERY WELL, DIP THE EGG IN WHITE VINEGAR FOR 15-30 SECONDS TO SOFTEN THE OUTER LAYER OF THE SHELL AND ALLOW THE DYE TO PENETRATE THE POROUS SURFACE MORE EASILY.

1 Close up the hole in the bottom of the egg (see page 124). Using a pencil, divide the egg into eight equal sections by drawing a horizontal and vertical line to create a cross, then adding four diagonal lines, as shown. Repeat on the other side of the egg, Making sure that the lines on both sides join up.

2 Add small guide marks halfway along each of the eight pencil lines on one side of the egg, then use the stylus pen and beeswax to create the outline of a star. Add a dot of beeswax to the centre of the egg where the eight pencil lines meet.

3 Draw a second star just inside the first one. Draw a line from the central dot toward each point of the second star, but don't let it touch the tip. Turn each line into a pine-tree branch by adding two rows of short lines that get slightly smaller as you move towards the end. Create a small flower shape around the beeswax dot by drawing pointed petals between the pine-tree branches. Repeat steps 2–3 on the other side of the egg, making sure that the tips of the stars meet neatly.

4 Turn the egg slightly and draw a series of small snowflakes in beeswax in the spaces between the tips of the stars by adding a small dot of beeswax where the pencil lines cross, then adding eight lines with smaller dots at the end. Continue until all the empty spaces are filled.

5 Submerge the egg in the light blue dye, leave for 10 minutes, then remove and blot dry with a paper towel. Use the stylus pen and beeswax to fill in the gap between the two star outlines and the small flower shape around the central beeswax dot. Repeat on the other side of the egg.

6 Submerge the egg in the dark blue dye, leaving it for long enough to ensure that you have a strong contrast between the two blue shades. Remove and blot dry with a clean paper towel. To reveal the design, hold the egg close to the candle flame and start removing the melting wax with a tissue (see page 125).

GOLD BLOCKED EGG

Colour Blocking with Tape

I had some painter's tape sitting on my desk and thought why not try using it to create a block pattern on an egg? You can position large bold strips of tape in any direction. Here, I used the tape to create the shape of a cross. I used gold acrylic paint, but you can be as imaginative as you like and use any metallic paint or any type of paint at all.

- One hollow brown chicken egg
- Painter's tape (any width as it can be cut to size)
- Scissors
- Gold acrylic paint
- Craft paintbrush
- Craft knife (optional)

1 My tape was a little too thick, so I cut it down the middle to make thinner strips. Stick two strips of tape to the egg, as if you are adding a couple of 'belts'. Add the first belt nearer the top of the egg and the second so that it runs round the length of the egg. Press the tape down neatly at the edges.

2 Using a small amount of gold acrylic, paint one section of the egg at a time and let dry.

3 Apply second and third coats of paint, letting the egg dry between each application, until the egg is completely covered with paint.

4 Check that the paint is thoroughly dry, then start peeling off the second strip of tape you applied. Then remove the first strip of tape.

5 Check the egg to see if it needs any touch-ups of paint. If the paint has seeped under the tape strips anywhere, use a craft knife to give the line a smoother edge.

COLOURFUL SPIDERS EGG

Beeswax and Three-colour Dye

This egg design is colourful and cheerful, calling to mind a summer garden full of flowers and cute bugs roaming around. These festive eggs would look great in a tall, clear, hurricane glass vase that's waiting to be filled with freshly cut flowers – they look like summer.

1 Close up the hole in the bottom of the egg (see page 124). Submerge the egg in the pink dye for 10 minutes or so, then remove and blot dry with a paper towel. Use the stylus pen to draw your first spider-like circle on the egg in beeswax.

2 Cover the whole egg with spider-like circles. If you are decorating more than one egg, change the scale of the circles to add more interest.

3 Submerge the egg in the yellow dyefor 10 minutes or so. Yellow dye is much lighter, but can wash off deep pinks and reds. Remove the egg from the dye and blot dry with a clean paper towel.

4 Use the stylus pen to fill in the circles with beeswax to preserve the yellow dye underneath.

2 Submerge the egg in the green dye for 10 minutes or so (or until you reach your desired shade of green). Again, remove the egg from the dye and blot dry with a clean paper towel.

3 To reveal the amazing colours, hold the egg close to the candle flame and start removing the melting wax with a tissue (see page 125). Keep turning the egg, holding it near the flame, and gently cleaning off the wax.

ZEBRA STRIPE EGG

Black-and-white Stripes

This simple, but striking-looking egg is inspired by trendy home décor designs. It makes a lovely ornament. It is easy to create and can be displayed all year round.

- One hollow white chicken egg
- Candle
- Lighter or matches
- Beeswax
- Hot-tip stylus pen (large size)

- Black eggshell dye
- Container with lid
- One teaspoon of white vinegar
- Teaspoon
- Paper towels

- Tissues
- Craft knife (optional)

1 Close up the hole in the bottom of the egg with beeswax (see page 124), then, working from the bottom to the top, start drawing flame-like shapes licking up the sides of the egg with beeswax and let dry.

2 Establish a good size for the flames and ensure the spaces between them are large enough to create the striped zebra effect.

3 Continue adding flames around the egg, checking that each one has a good coverage of beeswax.

4 Once the egg is covered with flames and the beeswax is dry, submerge in the black dye for 10 minutes or so. Remove the egg from the dye and blot dry with a paper towel.

5 Hold the egg close to the candle flame and start removing the melting wax with a tissue (see page 125). Keep turning the egg, holding it near the flame, gently cleaning off the wax. If necessary, use a craft knife to remove any black imperfections from the white parts of the design.

OAK-LEAF MOTIF EGG

Drawn Lines and Dripped Drops

The oak leaf is a common motif in folk art, and is also an easy shape to create. The oak-leaf brown and turquoise dyes used here produce a classic colour combination, suitable for the autumn, or perhaps as an autumn centrepiece, while a display of these eggs with little acorns would also be lovely.

- One hollow white chicken egg
- Candle
- Lighter or matches
- Hot-tip stylus pen (medium size)
- Beeswax

- Pencil
- Thin beeswax candle (as you would use for a birthday cake)
- Two eggshell dyes in turquoise and brown
- Two containers with lids

- Two teaspoons of white vinegar
- Two teaspoons
- Paper towels
- Tissues

1 Close up the hole in the bottom of the egg with beeswax (see page 124). Using a pencil, divide the egg into four equal sections from top to bottom, using parallel lines to create 'belts' around the egg.

2 Draw a wavy line in the middle of one of the four sections (adding a straight pencil line as a guide if you don't feel confident enough to do this freehand). Try to mimic the edge of an oak leaf when drawing the wavy line. Repeat for the remaining sections.

3 Draw evenly spaced dots, all the same size, in the four belts dividing the egg. Then fill in the oak-leaf shapes with thin, evenly spaced lines to create a striking contrast of bold dots and thin stripes.

4 Go over your linework with beeswax (see page 123), let dry, then submerge the egg in the turquoise dye. After 10 minutes or so, remove the egg from the dye and blot dry with a paper towel.

5 Light the thin candle, point it downwards, and start dripping drops of wax in one of the four sections. Let the wax dry before turning the egg and adding more drops of wax to the next section. Continue turning the egg and dripping the wax until all four sections are filled with drops.

6 Submerge the egg in the brown dye for 10 minutes or so, then remove and blot dry with a clean paper towel. Using the large candle, hold the egg close to the flame and start removing the melting wax with a tissue (see page 125). Keep turning the egg, holding it near the flame, and gently cleaning off the wax.

ABSTRACT LINES EGG

Single-colour Dye and Beeswax Sheets

This simple egg is ideal for smaller kids to make. The idea here is to create a fun and spontaneous craft moment with very few materials. Using beeswax honeycomb sheets produces a decorative pattern. Here, I opted for abstract smudges, but dots would look great too – simply cut the sheet of beeswax into circles rather than strips.

- One hollow white chicken egg
- Candle
- Lighter or matches
- Beeswax honeycomb sheet

- Scissors
- Yellow eggshell dye
- Container with lid
- One teaspoon of white vinegar

- Teaspoon
- Paper towels
- Tissues

1 Close up the hole in the bottom of the egg with beeswax (see page 124). Cut thin strips from the sheet of beeswax and start pressing them onto the egg.

2 As you press on the strips, the heat from your hand will help the wax adhere. Don't rush this stage and let the wax heat up in your hands.

3 Apply wax strips all over the egg in a criss-cross pattern. Using narrower strips of wax will give better results.

4 Once the strips are stuck down well, submerge the egg in the yellow dye and leave for 10 minutes or so. Remove the egg from the dye and blot dry with a paper towel.

5 To remove the strips, hold the egg close to the candle flame and start removing the melting wax with a tissue (see page 125). Keep turning the egg, holding it near the flame, gently cleaning off the wax.

TIP

YOU CAN MAKE EDIBLE VERSIONS OF THIS EGG, TOO. USE BAKER'S FOOD COLOURING OR MAKE A NATURAL DYE BY BOILING UP SOME DRY ONION SHELLS TO DECORATE HARDBOILED EGGS. YOU'LL ALSO NEED TO USE A NATURAL BEESWAX CANDLE.

CONFETTI EGG

Food-colour Polka Dots

This design reminds me of edible cake décor confetti, hence the name. These are fun eggs that kids can decorate without making a mess – and the best part is they can snack on them, too. If you have pale heritage chicken eggs or lighter brown ones, that will work as well – they might not mimic a vanilla cupcake top, but will still make for some fun family crafting and provide an edible snack.

• One white hardboiled chicken egg
• Cotton buds
• Food-colouring set
• Tissues

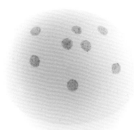

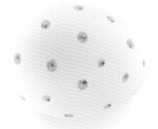

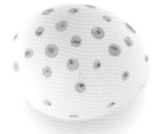

1 Let the hardboiled egg cool down. Dip a cotton bud in the opening of one of the food-coloring containers to wet it with your first colour (here, I used blue). Keeping the cotton bud at a 90-degree angle to the egg, start pressing dots over one side. The harder you press, the larger the dot will be, so start small and then make the dot larger if necessary.

2 Cover the whole egg in the first colour, letting each area dry before going on to the next. It can be helpful to use a tissue to hold the egg to avoid smudging the dots.

3 Take your second colour – in this case, green – and follow the same process to cover the egg in green dots.

4 Continue with your next colour. Here, I used red. If you wish, make these dots slightly larger so they stand out more.

5 Keep turning the egg, adding more dots in different colours. My final colour here is yellow. I had four colours in my set (blue, green, red and yellow), but three or five will work just as well.

TIP

IF YOU ARE ONLY USING TWO COLOURS, TRY PLAYING AROUND WITH THE SCALE AND SATURATION OF THE DOTS. THESE EGGS ARE SAFE TO EAT. YOU CAN PUT THEM ON DISPLAY, BUT THEY SHOULD BE EATEN BY THE END OF THE DAY. ALTERNATIVELY, THE EGGS WILL KEEP FOR A WEEK IN THE REFRIGERATOR.

PAPER CLIPS EGG

Random Overlapping Pattern

The inspiration for this design is back-to-school autumn colours, harvest time, Thanksgiving décor and falling leaves in shades varying from yellow to deep red. These are fun eggs to make with children, as they can mess up the pattern of the paper clips and the egg will still look good. Please note: Children should be supervised when working with candles and hot wax.

- One hollow white chicken egg
- Candle
- Lighter or matches
- Hot-tip stylus pen (medium size)
- Beeswax

- Three eggshell dyes in sunny yellow, orange and dark red
- Three containers with lids
- Three teaspoons of white vinegar
- Three teaspoons

- Paper towels
- Tissues

1 Close up the hole in the bottom of the egg (see page 124). Submerge the egg in the sunny yellow dye for 10 minutes or so, then remove and blot dry with a paper towel.

2 As this is a random pattern, you can draw directly on the egg with the stylus pen and beeswax. Starting on one side of the egg, draw slim ovals all over the surface.

3 Continue drawing the paper clips all over the egg. Don't be afraid to overlap them.

4 Submerge the egg in the orange dye for 10 minutes or so, then remove and blot dry with a clean paper towel.

5 Using the stylus pen and beeswax, add lots of micro-dots all over the egg, ensuring they are evenly spaced.

6 Dark red is your final color. Submerge the egg in the dark red dye for 10 minutes or so, then remove and blot dry with a clean paper towel. To finish, hold the egg close to the candle flame and start removing the melting wax with a tissue (see page 125). Keep turning the egg, holding it near the flame, gently cleaning off the wax.

BLACK-AND-RED KNITTED PATTERN EGG

Two-colour Dye and Winter Star

When I came up with the design for this egg, I was thinking about knitting a ski hat or something wintery and warm. Traditional eight-pointed stars are often seen in winter apparel. Ta-da! You now have a winter hat-inspired egg that would make a great gift or tree ornament.

- One hollow white chicken egg
- Pencil
- Candle
- Lighter or matches
- Hot-tip stylus pens (small and medium size)

- Beeswax
- Two eggshell dyes in red and black
- Two containers with lids
- Two teaspoons of white vinegar (for the dye), plus extra for etching
- Two teaspoons

- Paper towels
- Tissues
- Old drinking glass or jar
- Latex gloves
- Small toothbrush

1 Close up the hole in the bottom of the egg with beeswax (see page 124). Submerge the egg in the red dye for 10 minutes or so, then remove and blot dry with a paper towel. Then, with a small stylus pen, draw a 'belt' with two narrow borders at the top and bottom of the egg. Add a row of diamond shapes in the large space between the two belts and a row of triangles above both belts. Let dry.

2 Add a border to each diamond and then fill with the intricate pattern shown in the photograph. This is precise work and it may take a few moments for you to feel confident with the design, so use a pencil first and then go over your linework in beeswax (see page 123). Complex patterns always need a bit more attention.

3 Draw a small star at the top and bottom of the egg and add large dashes between the triangles. Fill in all the areas that are to remain red with beeswax, where shown. Use the medium stylus pen to speed up the process.

4 Immerse the egg in vinegar in the bottom of a drinking glass or jar. Leave for about 10 minutes or until the outer layer of shell starts to lift and shed. Keep turning the egg so that it comes into contact evenly with the vinegar. Wearing gloves, remove the egg from the vinegar and rinse in cold water, lightly brushing with a soft brush to remove the outer layer of shell.

5 Blot dry with a paper towel. It's fine if the eggshell looks slightly pink. I have used blue beeswax here to demonstrate this step more clearly, but you can just continue with the beeswax you have used so far. Simply fill in all the white parts with blue beeswax using the medium stylus pen.

6 Submerge the egg in the black dye for 10 minutes or so, then remove and blot dry with a clean paper towel. Hold the egg close to the candle flame and start removing the melting wax with a tissue (see page 125). Keep turning the egg, holding it near the flame, gently cleaning off the wax.

DIAGONAL GEOMETRIC EGG

Solid Bands and Zigzags

Children's toys like model sharks and dinosaurs usually have big teeth. This makes this egg great fun for a shark-lover or dinosaur fan! The dye used should be dark to contrast with the white egg and make the geometric lines stand out. I used purple here, but you could also use dark red or even black. This egg would look wonderful displayed in an egg stand on a bookshelf next to some dinosaur books.

YOU WILL NEED

- One hollow white chicken egg
- Candle
- Lighter or matches
- Hot-tip stylus pen (medium size)
- Beeswax

- Pencil
- Purple eggshell dye
- Container with lid
- One teaspoon of white vinegar
- Teaspoon

- Paper towels
- Tissues

1 Close up the hole in the bottom of the egg (see page 124). Divide the egg in half by drawing a pencil line on both sides from top to bottom. Draw more lines around the egg, but tilt them slightly to produce a row of diagonals. Make sure some of the lines are closer together to create thin and thick bands around the egg. Go over your linework with beeswax (see page 123) and leave to dry.

2 Once you have a good number of lines, start filling in some of the bands with beeswax and some with small triangles that mimic shark's teeth. Ideally, the filled-in bands should be in the middle of the egg, but are useful in places where you have made a mistake and your line is crooked.

3 Add further visual interest by drawing a row of triangles resembling arrowheads along a pencil line, then go over your linework with beeswax.

4 Finally, fill one or two of the thinner bands at the top and bottom of the egg with beeswax.

5 Submerge the egg in the purple dye for 10 minutes or so, then remove and blot dry with a paper towel. To finish, hold the egg close to the candle flame and start removing the melting wax with a tissue (see page 125).

TIP

YOU CAN REMOVE PENCIL MARKS FROM THE SURFACE OF THE EGG AS YOU WOULD FROM PAPER. USE A CRAFT KNIFE TO SCRAPE OFF BEESWAX IF YOU MAKE A MISTAKE.

VINEGAR-ETCHED BROWN EGG

Acid Etching with Vinegar

The technique used to create this egg is called acid etching or washing back. I love displaying vinegar-etched eggs in a dry floral arrangement in a shallow wicker basket on a vintage doily on a rustic table. The stronger the vinegar used, the faster it will work on the egg. Here, I've used two beeswax colours to show the steps clearly, but you can use any beeswax you have.

TIP

IF THIS DESIGN SEEMS DIFFICULT, BEGIN WITH AN EASIER PATTERN TO TEST YOUR SKILLS. EVEN A STRAIGHTFORWARD POLKA-DOT DESIGN WILL DEMONSTRATE HOW VINEGAR ETCHING WORKS.

YOU WILL NEED

- One hollow brown chicken egg
- Candle
- Lighter or matches
- Hot-tip stylus pens (medium and large size)

- Beeswax
- Pencil
- Old drinking glass or jar
- White vinegar
- Latex gloves

- Small toothbrush
- Paper towels
- Tissues

1 Close up the hole in the bottom of the egg with beeswax (see page 124). Using a pencil, create guidelines for the lattice pattern by drawing a series of diamond shapes around the egg. You'll probably be able to fit in about four diamonds. Go over your linework with the medium stylus pen and black beeswax (see page 123) and let dry.

2 Draw an eight-petalled flower inside each diamond and fill in four of the petals with beeswax. Include a dot in the centre of the flowers and add decorative lines with a dot at the end to the other petals. Use the medium stylus pen to draw the outline of the design and the large stylus pen to fill in with beeswax.

3 Add another diamond shape to the top and bottom of the egg. Add a border around each diamond shape by drawing a second diamond around the first one. Fill in the diamonds at the top and bottom of the egg with flowers, as before. Also fill each diamond border with a series of evenly spaced lines. Let dry.

4 Immerse the egg in vinegar in the bottom of a drinking glass or jar. Leave for 20–40 minutes or until the outer layer of brown shell starts to lift and shed. Keep turning the egg so that it comes into contact evenly with the vinegar. Wearing gloves, remove the egg from the vinegar and rinse in cold water, lightly brushing with a soft brush to remove the outer layer of brown shell. Blot dry with a paper towel.

5 Using the red beeswax to help you keep track, add further embellishments to the design. I added a solid border to the diamonds and a series of zigzagging parallel lines. I also filled in the empty petals of the flowers and added more decorative lines with dots.

6 Return the egg to the vinegar to bring the shell another shade closer to white. Again, rinse the vinegar off the egg and pat dry with a paper towel. Hold the egg close to the candle flame and start removing the melting wax with a tissue (see page 125). Keep turning the egg, holding it near the flame, gently cleaning off the wax.

TEAL TWIGS EGG

Organic Twigs on Teal

This simple egg design reminds me of very early spring when the garden is still brown and the buds on the trees are only just starting to swell. This rustic egg, with its folk-art-inspired design, would look wonderful displayed in a wicker or straw basket.

TIP

IF YOU WOULD LIKE YOUR EGG TO HAVE A DARKER TEAL COLOUR, THEN USE A DARKER EGG.

- One hollow brown chicken egg
- Candle
- Lighter or matches
- Hot-tip stylus pen (medium size)
- Beeswax

- Pencil
- Turquoise eggshell dye
- Container with lid
- One teaspoon of white vinegar
- Teaspoon

- Paper towels
- Tissues

1 Close up the hole in the bottom of the egg (see page 124). Using a pencil, draw two twigs shooting up from the bottom.

2 Moving towards the top of the egg, draw two more twigs, but slant them slightly to make the design look more organic.

3 Continue drawing more twigs in this way until you've covered the whole egg. Go over your linework with beeswax (see page 123) and let dry.

4 Submerge the egg in the turquoise dye and leave for 10 minutes or so. The turquoise dye will give your egg its teal colour. Remove the egg from the dye and blot dry with a paper towel.

5 To finish, hold the egg close to the candle flame and start removing the melting wax with a tissue (see page 125). Keep turning the egg, holding it near the flame, gently cleaning off the wax.

BLACK AND SILVER MARKED EGG

Single-colour Dye with Silver Marker

The simple elegance of this egg is matched by the fact that it's also easy to make. It is perfect for a simple home décor, being black with metallic silver accenting. A group of these eggs would look great on display in a silver, sculpture-like tray shaped like a leaf, for example.

TIP

TRY MAKING MORE EGGS, VARYING THE PATTERN SO YOU HAVE A MIXTURE OF DESIGNS, INCLUDING SILVER LINES, POLKA DOTS, SWIRLS AND SOLID AREAS.

- One hollow chicken egg (any colour is fine)
- Candle
- Lighter or matches
- Hot-tip stylus pen (medium size)
- Beeswax

- Pencil
- Black eggshell dye
- One container with lid
- One teaspoon of white vinegar
- Teaspoon

- Paper towels
- Silver marker pen (with a medium tip)

1 Close up the hole in the bottom of the egg with beeswax (see page 124). Submerge the egg in the black dye for 10 minutes or so, then remove and blot dry with a paper towel.

2 Use a pencil to divide the egg into eight equal sections from top to bottom, then, go over your linework with the silver marker pen.

3 Draw a line with the marker pen around the middle of the egg. If you wish, use the pencil to mark this first and then go over the line with the pen.

4 You should now have 16 sections. Start drawing evenly spaced lines with the marker pen in every other section. (Alternatively, you could fill some of the sections solid silver.)

5 Continue to work around the egg, filling alternate sections with evenly spaced lines.

6 Add branch-like swirls to the empty black sections. An alternative here would be to add polka dots instead.

TURQUOISE AND RED EGG

Simple Red Daisy Motif

The garden daisy makes a bold design statement and is probably the very first flower in everyone's life. Kids love this egg design. Although I positioned daisies on the four sides and also top and bottom here, randomly placed flowers would look great too.

- One hollow white chicken egg
- Candle
- Lighter or matches
- Hot-tip stylus pen (large size)

- Beeswax
- Two eggshell dyes in red and turquoise
- Two containers with lids
- Two teaspoons of white vinegar

- Two teaspoons
- Paper towels
- Tissues

1 Close up the hole in the bottom of the egg (see page 124). Submerge the egg in the red dye for 10 minutes or so, then remove and blot dry with a paper towel. Add a dot of beeswax to the middle of one side of the egg, then draw four teardrop-shaped petals around the dot.

2 Create a daisy by adding more petals around the beeswax dot, keeping them the same length and the same distance apart – imagine you are creating a perfect imaginary circle.

3 Continue adding dots and petals in beeswax until you have a daisy on the top and bottom of the egg and on the remaining three sides.

4 Submerge the egg in the turquoise dye and leave until the red colour in the spaces between the daisies is no longer visible – this may take longer than usual. Remove from the dye and blot dry with a clean paper towel.

5 To finish, hold the egg close to the candle flame and start removing the melting wax with a tissue (see page 125). Keep turning the egg, holding it near the flame, gently cleaning off the wax.

TIP

USE SOME WHITE VINEGAR ON A PAPER TOWEL TO WASH OFF THE RED IN THE SPACES BETWEEN THE DAISIES AFTER STEP 4 IF YOU WOULD LIKE AN EGG THAT'S A VERY LIGHT COLOUR.

YOU MAY WANT TO PRACTISE DRAWING THE TEARDROP SHAPE THAT FORMS THE PETALS OF THE DAISIES IN PENCIL ON A PIECE OF PAPER FIRST.

BLACK AND YELLOW CONTRAST EGG

Two-colour Dye with Geometric Pattern

This egg is perfect for anyone who likes their skills challenged – you need both patience and good eyesight. I created this egg just for this book, as I wanted to offer a variety of designs that would appeal to everyone. I've even seen teenage boys and girls have a go at this one. This is a super-stylish, modern egg that has room in the empty 'belts' for you to write customized text.

- One hollow white chicken egg
- Candle
- Lighter or matches
- Hot-tip stylus pen (large size)
- Beeswax

- Pencil
- Two eggshell dyes in black and yellow
- Two containers with lids
- Two teaspoons of white vinegar (for the dye), plus extra for etching
- Two teaspoons

- Paper towels
- Tissues
- Old drinking glass or jar
- Latex gloves
- Small toothbrush

1 Close up the hole in the bottom of the egg with beeswax (see page 124). Submerge the egg in the black dye for 10 minutes or so, then remove and blot dry with a paper towel. Use a pencil to divide the egg into four equal sections, from top to bottom, by using parallel lines to create two 'belts' around the egg. Then draw another belt around the middle of the egg. Go over your linework with black beeswax (see page 123) and let dry.

2 Draw two closely spaced parallel lines in black beeswax in each of the eight sections and then fill these with a series of evenly spaced lines. Ensure that the lines in each section are nice and uniform. Fill in the squares where the belts cross with beeswax.

3 Immerse the egg in vinegar in the bottom of a drinking glass or jar. Leave for 10 minutes or until the outer layer of shell starts to lift and shed. Keep turning the egg so that it comes into contact evenly with the vinegar. Wearing gloves, remove the egg and rinse in cold water, lightly brushing with a soft brush to remove the outer layer of shell. Blot dry.

4 Fill the belts with red beeswax to preserve the light colour underneath. Do not fill the squares where the belts cross, as these will remain black. Submerge the egg in the yellow dye for 10 minutes or so, then remove and blot dry with a clean paper towel.

5 Hold the egg close to the candle flame and start removing the melting wax with a tissue (see page 125). Keep turning the egg, holding it near the flame and gently cleaning off the wax.

TEACUP CORNFLOWER EGG

Floral and Leaf Painting

Inspiration for this egg comes from the patterns found on vintage teacups, old china and dinnerware. I think these eggs look beautiful displayed with the Green Grass Egg (see page 104). For this project, I used a children's face-painting kit, which means the paints are safe and non-toxic.

- One hollow white chicken egg
- Children's face-painting kit or acrylic/ watercolour paint set (with a selection of paintbrushes with thin tips)

1 Moisten a medium-size paintbrush with blue paint. Then, working on one side of the egg, begin painting a circle of petals to create a cornflower. Make the petals small to begin with and then bigger if necessary. Repeat on the other side of the egg, so you have two cornflower designs.

2 Switch to a smaller paintbrush and, using some purple paint, draw a series of teardrop shapes to create a fern-like leaf.

3 Repeat step 2 using the same smaller paintbrush (remember to clean it first), but this time with some light blue paint.

4 Keep painting fern-like leaves around the cornflower, alternating between purple and light blue.

5 Ensure the egg is covered with leaves and let dry. Fill the centre of the cornflowers with light blue, then add a large dot of purple paint, letting the paint dry between each application.

6 Brighten up the egg further by adding some leaves in bright green. Once the egg is dry, add a second coat of blue to the cornflowers to intensify their colour.

SIMPLE ORGANIC PATTERN EGG

Folk-art Tree Motif

The simple organic pattern on this egg is reminiscent of that seen on primitive folk-art eggs. It includes various traditional elements of folk-art drawings, including dots, swirls and twigs. This rustic egg is also inspired by the colours of autumn and by naked trees that have only a few leaves still hanging. Try displaying this egg in a black straw basket as part of an autumn home décor.

TIP

AS BROWN EGGS TAKE LONGER TO ABSORB
DYE, YOU CAN SPEED UP THE PROCESS BY
WORKING WITH LIGHTER SHADES OF
BROWN EGGS.

YOU WILL NEED

- One hollow light brown chicken egg
- Candle
- Lighter or matches
- Hot-tip stylus pen (medium size)
- Beeswax
- Pencil
- Two eggshell dyes in orange and pink
- Two containers with lids
- Two teaspoons of white vinegar
- Two teaspoons
- Paper towels
- Tissues

1 Close up the hole in the bottom of the egg (see page 124). In pencil, draw two parallel lines from top to bottom on one side of the egg. Add a row of swirls sprouting on both sides of the lines, as shown.

2 Draw three more sets of parallel lines, again working from the top of the egg to the bottom, so you have four equal sections divided by 'belts' running around the egg. Add more rows of swirls on each side of the belts. Go over your linework with beeswax (see page 123) and let dry.

3 Before dyeing with the first colour, dip the egg in white vinegar for about 30 seconds to remove a thin layer of shell – brown eggs take colour more slowly, so this will speed things up. Submerge the egg in the orange dye for 10 minutes or so, then remove and blot dry with a paper towel.

4 Using the stylus pen and beeswax, add rows of large dots in the empty space in each section. Make these dots nice and bold. Then fill in all the belts with beeswax.

5 Submerge the egg in the pink dye. Let the egg sit for a while to ensure the pink dye is absorbed. The pink will look almost burgundy on the brown eggshell. Remove the egg from the dye and blot dry with a clean paper towel.

6 To finish, hold the egg close to the candle flame and start removing the melting wax with a tissue (see page 125). Keep turning the egg, holding it near the flame, gently cleaning off the wax.

SCOTTISH TREASURE EGG

Patterns in Tartan

The distinctive pattern of Scottish tartan is well known – think of tartan textiles, gift wrap and furniture upholstery, as well as a tartan grandpa chair, grandma apron and tablecloth. Tartan feels both homely and very familiar. Although this tartan egg design is easy and fun to do, it will test the steadiness of your hands as your draw the lines!

TIP

WHEN DRAWING THE BEESWAX LINES, MAKE SOME THICKER OR ADD MORE OF THEM IF YOU'D LIKE A PARTICULAR COLOUR TO STAND OUT IN THE FINAL DESIGN. IF YOU MAKE A MISTAKE WHEN DRAWING IN THE BEESWAX, JUST THICKEN THE LINE AND MAKE IT BOLDER, AS IF THIS WAS YOUR INTENTION.

- One hollow white chicken egg
- Candle
- Lighter or matches
- Hot-tip stylus pen (medium size)
- Beeswax

- Pencil
- Three eggshell dyes in yellow, green and red
- Three containers with lids
- Three teaspoons of white vinegar

- Three teaspoons
- Paper towels
- Tissues

1 Close up the hole in the bottom of the egg (see page 124). Using a pencil, draw a horizontal and a vertical line on one side of the egg to create a cross, then adding two more vertical lines on either side of the vertical central line. Repeat on the other side of the egg, making sure that the lines on both sides join up. On both sides, draw two curved lines from the top to the bottom of the egg, both above and below the central horizontal line. Go over your linework with black and blue beeswax (see page 123). Let dry.

2 Submerge the egg in the yellow dye for 10 minutes or so, remove and blot dry with a paper towel. Draw a second line close to some of the horizontal and vertical lines, to start creating the tartan pattern. Go over your line work with beeswax,. Let dry.

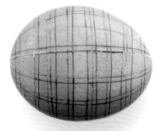

3 Submerge the egg in the green dye for 10 minutes or so, then remove and blot dry with a clean paper towel.

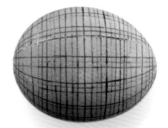

4 Draw more horizontal and vertical lines in beeswax (to preserve the green colour underneath) and let dry.

5 Red is your last colour. Before dyeing, check that the egg is well filled with lines and that there are no large gaps between any lines. You can also double the thickness of some lines to add more impact. Submerge the egg in the red dye for 10 minutes or so, then remove and blot dry, as before.

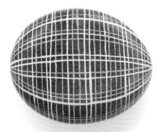

6 To finish, hold the egg close to the candle flame and start removing the melting wax with a tissue (see page 125). Keep turning the egg, holding it near the flame, gently cleaning off the wax.

BLUE VINEGAR-ETCHED EGG

Acid Etching and One-colour Dye

This egg produces a monochromatic look. It is perfect if you like white eggs dyed blue, but you are adding a little twist by reversing the colour and having white eggs with a blue pattern. As with the Vinegar-etched Brown Egg (see page 72), this egg is washed back to white or acid-etched – I like to use vinegar-etching terminology. I love this egg as a baby boy's keepsake or to celebrate a first seaside holiday, or as a cute nursery ornament in a silver stand.

TIP
_____
UNLIKE FOR BROWN EGGS, YOU DON'T
NEED A STRONG ACID SUCH AS
VINEGAR, BUT CAN USE SOME LEMON
JUICE INSTEAD.

- One hollow white chicken egg
- Candle
- Lighter or matches
- Hot-tip stylus pen (medium size)
- Beeswax

- Pencil
- Turquoise eggshell dye
- Container with lid
- One teaspoon of white vinegar (for the dye), plus extra for etching

- Teaspoon
- Paper towels and tissues
- Old drinking glass or jar
- Latex gloves
- Small toothbrush

1 Close up the hole in the bottom of the egg with beeswax (see page 124). Submerge the egg in the turquoise dye and leave for 10 minutes or so, then remove and blot dry. Divide the egg into four equal sections from top to bottom. Add double lines around the top and bottom of the egg and connect them with four evenly spaced sets of vertical double lines. Go over your linework in beeswax (see page 123). Let dry, then fill in the four vertical bands with rows of small diamonds.

2 Add a further row of solid diamonds followed by a narrow border above the bands at the top and bottom of the egg. Then draw another large diamond in the spaces top and bottom, and fill with a symmetrical pattern of squares and triangles.

3 Add a large double diamond to the spaces between the vertical bands all around the egg.

4 Fill the inside of the empty diamonds with a symmetrical pattern of squares and triangles. Take your time here, as this is precision work. Check the egg to make sure you are happy with the design, and fill in any gaps.

5 Immerse the egg in vinegar in the bottom of a drinking glass or jar. Leave for about 10 minutes or until the outer layer of shell starts to lift and shed. Keep turning the egg so that it comes into contact evenly with the vinegar. Wearing gloves, remove the egg from the vinegar and rinse in cold water, lightly brushing with a soft brush to remove the outer layer of shell. Blot dry with a paper towel.

6 Hold the egg close to the candle flame and start removing the melting wax with a tissue (see page 125). Keep turning the egg, holding it near the flame, gently cleaning off the wax.

ORANGE AND LILAC BOTANICAL EGG

Two-colour Dye and Botanical Pattern

I love this colour combination – I would like to have a blouse with a pattern like this! I enjoy combining pink, lilac, purple and orange. My garden is just about to bloom with purple hyacinths and lilac. I have a number of irises in a variety of colours, from salmon-orange to rich purples. I often try to mix dyes to mimic the flowers in my garden. When my garden is in flower, I find myself inventing many new patterns. It provides natural inspiration.

- One hollow white chicken egg
- Candle
- Lighter or matches
- Hot-tip stylus pen (medium size)
- Beeswax
- Pencil

- Two eggshell dyes in purple and orange
- Two containers with lids
- Two teaspoons of white vinegar, plus extra for etching
- Two teaspoons
- Paper towels

- Tissues
- Old drinking glass or jar (for the etching vinegar)
- Latex gloves
- Small toothbrush

1 Close up the hole in the bottom of the egg with beeswax (see page 124). Submerge the egg in the purple dye for 10 minutes or so, then remove and blot dry with a paper towel. Use a pencil to divide the egg into six equal sections from top to bottom, then go over your linework with beeswax (see page 123) and let dry.

2 Draw rows of leaves on either side of every other line, establishing the scale of the leaves. Let dry.

3 Immerse the egg in vinegar in the bottom of a drinking glass or jar. Leave for about 10 minutes or until the outer layer of shell starts to lift and shed. Keep turning the egg so that it comes into contact evenly with the vinegar. Keep the shade of lilac, but ensure it is light enough for the orange to be visible later. Wearing gloves, remove the egg from the vinegar and rinse in cold water, lightly brushing with a soft brush to remove the outer layer of shell. Blot dry with a paper towel.

4 Fill the leaves with beeswax and embellish the remaining empty lines with a row of dots on either side.

5 Submerge the egg in the orange dye and leave for 10 minutes or so. If you don't like the shade of orange, give the egg another 'wash back' in vinegar until it is lighter.

6 Hold the egg close to the candle flame and start removing the melting wax with a tissue (see page 125). Keep turning the egg, holding it near the flame, gently cleaning off the wax.

GOLD CHEVRON EGG

Gold Marker on White

This is a simple and elegant design. Inspired by a white silky blouse with bold golden stripes, this egg makes for the perfect table setting. Create several and place them in an elegant white platter in the middle of the table to impress guests. They are sure to be a big talking point!

YOU WILL NEED

- One white chicken egg, hollow, full or hardboiled (depending on the age of the crafter)
- Fine-tip permanent gold ink marker pen

1 Start by dividing the egg into four sections from top to bottom.

2 Divide each of the four sections to create eight. To avoid smudges, let the egg dry in between applying the lines.

3 Once the egg is divided into eight even sections, start adding the diagonal lines in the first section in the middle of the egg.

4 Move to the section next to it, adding lines in the opposite direction. Work around the top half of the egg first, changing the direction of the diagonal lines in each section.

5 Once the top half is dry, repeat steps 3 and 4 on the bottom half of the egg.

BLUE POLKA-DOT EGG

Polka Dots

This is the simplest egg you can make, so it's a great one for the kids to do. Use hardboiled eggs, which are easier for little ones to handle, and a highlighter or non-toxic marker pen. Once complete, use the eggs to create an egg-citing egg hunt in your garden – what a way to spend a fun-filled afternoon with the kids!

YOU WILL NEED

- One white chicken egg, hollow, full or hardboiled (depending on the age of the crafter)
- Blue highlighter pen
- Tissues

1 Make a big polka dot in the centre of the egg.

2 Add more big polka dots, keeping the spacing between each consistent.

3 Continue adding dots, working on one area at a time and allowing each area to dry before turning the egg. To speed up the drying time, blot the egg with tissues.

4 To add visual interest and variety, add some tiny dots between the bigger polka dots.

SWEDISH COUNTRY EGG

Single-colour Dye and Acrylic Paint

This simple but classic design is inspired by blue and yellow home décor, blue skies and fields of wild flowers.
A collection of these eggs would look great displayed on a small table in a white, country-style home.

- One hollow white chicken egg
- Candle
- Lighter or matches
- Hot-tip stylus pen (medium size)
- Beeswax

- Pencil
- Blue eggshell dye
- Container with lid
- One teaspoon of white vinegar
- Teaspoon

- Paper towels
- Yellow acrylic paint
- Craft paintbrush with a soft pointed tip

1 Close up the hole in the bottom of the egg with beeswax (see page 124). Start by submerging the egg in the blue dye and leaving for 10 minutes or so. Remove the egg from the dye and blot dry with a paper towel. Then use a pencil to divide the egg into six equal sections from top to bottom. These will be your guidelines.

2 Dip the paintbrush in the yellow paint and start adding a line of petals along the first guideline. Establish the scale of the petals and make sure they are all facing in the same direction.

3 Continue adding more petals along the other side of the guideline, letting the paint dry between applications.

4 Keep adding more petals on either side of the guideline and applying extra coats so that the yellow petals stand out.

5 Repeat steps 2–4 until you have painted petals along both sides of the remaining five guidelines.

6 Check the top of the egg and add more petals as necessary so that all the lines meet neatly. Go over any petals that need more paint. Let dry.

HOT PINK AND BLACK FLOWER EGG

Single-colour Dye and Acrylic Paint

The striking design for this egg, with its bold pink background, is inspired by a textile design microprint on a shirt.

YOU WILL NEED

- One hollow white chicken egg
- Candle
- Lighter or matches
- Beeswax
- Hot-tip stylus pen (medium size)

- Pink eggshell dye
- Container with lid
- One teaspoon of white vinegar
- Teaspoon
- Paper towels

- Black and white acrylic paints
- Craft paintbrush with a soft pointed tip

1 Close up the hole in the bottom of the egg with beeswax (see page 124). Submerge the egg in the pink dye and leave for 10 minutes or so. Remove the egg from the dye and blot dry with a paper towel.

2 Dip the paintbrush in the black paint and start painting a circle of petals on one side of the egg to create the first black flower. Establish the scale of the flowers at this stage.

3 Check you are happy with the size of the first flower and make it slightly larger if you wish.

4 Continue adding more flowers all over the egg, letting the paint dry before turning and working on the next section.

5 Don't worry about counting the number of petals for each flower, as they will look great at the end even if this is not precise. Add a tiny dot of white paint to the centre of each flower.

HERRINGBONE EGG

Black Ink Herringbone

This egg design is so simple, yet so beautiful. Inspired by shapes in nature, it is a universal piece. The best thing about it is that you do not need to get lots of art supplies. All you need is an egg from the fridge and a black marker pen from the drawer.

YOU WILL NEED

- One white chicken egg, hollow, full or hardboiled (depending on the age of the crafter)
- Fine-tip permanent black ink marker pen

1 Start by dividing the egg into four sections from top to bottom. Then, divide each of the four sections to create eight.

2 Once the egg is divided into eight even sections, start adding diagonal lines to your first section in the middle of the egg. Move on to the section next to it, adding lines in the opposite direction.

3 To avoid smudges as you move around the egg, fill in two sections at a time and allow to dry before moving on to the next two sections.

5 Repeat steps 2–3 until all eight sections are filled in.

4 Make the dividing lines thicker to complete your design.

PINK STRIPE EGG

Tonal Stripes

Inspired by candy stripes, fuchsia flowers and ribbons in girls' hair, this design is bold and festive. Use in egg hunts at Easter time, create a colourful egg bouquet for Mother's Day or display as decorations for spring birthdays.

YOU WILL NEED

- One white chicken egg, hollow, full or hardboiled (depending on the age of the crafter)
- Fine-tip permanent ink marker pen in two different shades of pink – one dark, one light

1 With the light pink marker, draw a thin line in the middle of the egg. Continue adding thin lines towards the top of the egg, varying the spacing between the lines.

2 Fill in the spaces between each line, changing the thickness and working from light to dark towards the top of the egg.

3 To finish the top half of the egg, draw and fill in a large dot on the very top of the egg.

4 Repeat steps 1–3 on the bottom half of the egg.

GREEN GRASS EGG

Feathered Paint Effect

I can't stress enough how much I love these simple eggs. I am planning to use them as mini vases on a large tray covered with moss. These eggs would also look lovely displayed on their own in a glass bowl. The paintbrush you use is important here, as it needs to be poor-quality with bristles that stick out and separate as you paint to achieve the 'grass' effect.

YOU WILL NEED

- One hollow white chicken egg
- Children's paint set (including a paintbrush)

1 Moisten, but don't wet, the paintbrush with some green paint. Then, starting at the bottom, begin running the brush up the egg, playing with a combination of shorter and longer strokes.

2 By using a small amount of paint and pressing the brush against the egg, the bristles will separate out and create the desired effect.

3 Work on one section of the egg at a time and let dry before turning the egg and applying more paint to the next section. Ensure the egg is covered with blades of grass.

4 Check the bottom of the egg to see if any areas need touching up with paint. Apply a second coat of paint to give definition to the thickness of some of the blades of grass. Let dry.

TIP

IF YOU PLAN TO USE THE EGGS AS MINI VASES, MAKE A LARGE OPENING IN THE TOP. ENSURE THE EGGS ARE WASHED WELL INSIDE TO AVOID SMELLY FLORAL ARRANGEMENTS.

NATIVITY SCENE EGG

Single-colour Dye and Illustration

My red-and-black Nativity egg is the most popular all year round. I have been making Nativity eggs for years now. Sometimes I make the design more complex, using an array of colours such as orange-red and burgundy, but this red egg is simple and very beautiful. Here, I used beeswax in two colours to demonstrate the steps more clearly. Why not hang this egg as an ornament, display it in a gold stand, or place it in a cluster of snowflake eggs with the same background colour?

TIP

IF YOU USE A BROWN EGG INSTEAD OF A WHITE ONE, IT CAN BE VINEGAR-ETCHED FOR A MORE RUSTIC FARMHOUSE LOOK.

YOU WILL NEED

- One hollow white chicken egg
- Candle
- Lighter or matches
- Hot-tip stylus pens (small and large size)

- Beeswax
- Pencil
- Red eggshell dye
- Container with lid
- One teaspoon of white vinegar

- One teaspoon
- Paper towels
- Tissues

1 Close up the hole in the bottom of the egg with beeswax (see page 124). Using a pencil, draw two T-shaped 'belts' from the top to the bottom. The horizontal part of the T-shapes should sit about a quarter of the way up from the bottom of the egg. The vertical parts should run all the way round. Add a narrow border to the inside of the vertical parts and above the horizontal part. Decorate the belts with leafy tendrils and rows of diamonds. Add a further diamond-filled border above the horizontal part of the T-shapes. Go over your linework with black beeswax (see page 123) using the small stylus pen, then use the large stylus pen to fill in the areas shown in the photograph. Let dry.

2 Add crosshatched areas to the vertical parts of the belts. Fill the diamonds with dots of red beeswax. Draw a star or snowflake on the bottom of the egg and add a crosshatched area around it. The idea here is to fill up all the empty spaces. You could also put a date or some words in this space if you're customizing the egg as a gift or for a special occasion.

3 In the narrow spaces between the vertical parts of the belts, draw a series of leaves in red beeswax. Bring the leaves to the top of the egg. Imagine that this will be an ornament with an attachment at the top.

4 In the wide spaces between the vertical parts of the belts, draw a Nativity scene, including a stable, Mary, Joseph, the Baby Jesus and a star (with four long and four short points). Add a couple of palm trees on either side of the stable. Switch stylus pens as necessary for the scene to draw thin and thick lines.

5 Submerge the egg in the red dye and leave for 10 minutes or so. Remove the egg from the dye and blot dry with a paper towel. Hold the egg close to the candle flame and start removing the melting wax with a tissue (see page 125). Keep turning the egg, holding it near the flame, gently cleaning off the wax.

BLACK-AND-WHITE SNOWFLAKE EGG

White-on-Black Snowflake Motif

Black and white fabrics, lace trims and textiles are always popular in interiors. In fact, a black-and-white design is suitable for both a rustic farmhouse and an elegant city home. A collection of these eggs looks fantastic on display in a rustic ceramic bowl on a crocheted doily. You could also turn these eggs into hanging ornaments – they would look great hanging from a tree with crocheted snowflakes.

- One hollow white chicken egg
- Candle
- Lighter or matches
- Hot-tip stylus pen (medium size)

- Beeswax
- Pencil
- Black eggshell dye
- Container with lid

- One teaspoon of white vinegar
- Teaspoon
- Paper towels
- Tissues

1 Close up the hole in the bottom of the egg (see page 124). Using a pencil, divide the egg into eight equal sections by drawing a horizontal and vertical line to create a cross, then adding four diagonal lines. Repeat on the other side of the egg, making sure the lines on both sides join up. On both sides, draw a dot where all the lines cross in the centre, then add a circle of eight petals to create a daisy shape. Go over your linework with beeswax (see page 123), drawing the lines boldly so they stand out, and let dry.

2 Continue to embellish the two daisy shapes, adding swirls and straight lines that fan out in the same direction like a windmill. To create the snowflake motif, draw the outline of a star around the 'windmills' on both sides of the egg.

3 To make the snowflakes more ornate, use the stylus pen and beeswax to fill the inside of the two stars with leaf-like shapes, then draw another star outline around the first and edge it with a series of tiny loops – think of these as a lace trim.

4 Turn the egg slightly and fill in the empty spaces between the points of the stars with more details to make the design look like a fancy doily. Here, each space has been filled with a simple cross and small daisy. Let the beeswax dry.

5 Once both snowflakes are drawn and all the sections filled in, submerge the egg in the black dye for 10 minutes or so, then remove and blot dry with a paper towel.

6 Hold the egg close to the candle flame and start removing the melting wax with a tissue (see page 125). Keep turning the egg, holding it near the flame and gently cleaning off the wax.

VINEGAR-ETCHED EGG

Floral and Leaf Pattern

Taking inspiration from textiles and home décor, beading designs and floral fashion fabrics, this egg is one of my favourites. The egg has a pattern that suggests the floral design of a fabric for a dress. The gorgeous flower motif would look fantastic on a batik silk scarf or blouse. For this project, I used blue and red beeswax to help keep the design clear, but you can use beeswax in any colour.

TIP

THE DARKER THE SHADE OF EGG YOU USE, THE STRONGER THE VINEGAR WILL NEED TO BE AND THE LONGER IT WILL NEED TO SIT IN THE VINEGAR.

- One hollow brown chicken egg
- Candle
- Lighter or matches
- Hot-tip stylus pen (medium size)
- Beeswax
- Old drinking glass or jar

- Latex gloves
- Small toothbrush
- Turquoise eggshell dye
- Container with lid
- One teaspoon of white vinegar (for the dye), plus extra for etching
- Teaspoon

- Paper towels
- Tissues

1 Close up the hole in the bottom of the egg (see page 124). Use the stylus pen and beeswax to draw a random pattern of flowers and leaves all over the egg.

2 Once the egg is well covered with your floral and leaf pattern, immerse it in vinegar in the bottom of a drinking glass or jar. Leave for 20–40 minutes or until the outer layer of brown shell starts to lift and shed. Keep turning the egg so that it comes into contact evenly with the vinegar.

3 Keep checking the egg to see if you are getting a much lighter shade – if you would like your egg to be lighter turquoise, use the acid etching to make the shell almost white. Wearing gloves, remove the egg from the vinegar and rinse in cold water, lightly brushing with a soft brush to remove the outer layer of brown shell.

4 Wash the egg and blot dry with a paper towel. Using the stylus pen and beeswax (I used red beeswax), fill in the leaves and outline the flowers.

5 Submerge the egg in the turquoise dye for 10 minutes or so, then remove and blot dry with a paper towel.

6 Hold the egg close to the candle flame and start removing the melting wax with a tissue (see page 125). Keep turning the egg, holding it near the flame and gently cleaning off the wax.

2/SHOWCASING YOUR EGGS · TECHNIQUES

SHOWCASING YOUR EGG ART

Now you've made a whole host of awesome egg art, it's time to put your projects to good use. Display them around your home as a celebratory centrepiece, table setting or Easter wreath. Or why not give them as a gift in the form of pretty planters or outstanding ornaments? What can you do with your egg art?

Welcome to the Table
Sometimes the simplest ideas can have the most impact. For any springtime celebration, dye your eggs in blush pink and pale blues and use a waterproof fibre tip to draw a simple face. Add bunny ears with a tied napkin.

Wonderful Wreath
Eggs of different sizes can be hot glued
to a circular structure and intertwined
with foliage to create a wonderful
wreath perfect for welcoming visitors
to your door.

Clutch of Eggs

What a rich and sumptuous display of highly burnished eggs! Put the prettiest ones on top and pile the plainer ones beneath to really pack a punch.

Mini Egg Flower Pots

Take the tops off the eggs and empty out the contents before rinsing. Fill with compost, then sow seeds or plant seedlings or simply use them as a support for spring blossoms.

Laying the Table
Dress up a table setting with brightly coloured eggs. Choose napkins to tone with the painted egg colour scheme.

Feather Your Nest
This neat display of batik-style eggs makes the perfect centrepiece for your table. Rest your creations in a nest-style bowl and use feathers as accents.

Eggstravaganza
Embellished, bejewelled and beribboned, mass your eggs together and display them as hanging ornaments. For maximum impact, don't hold back on the decoration.

TECHNIQUES

When decorating eggs, there are some techniques that crop up again and again. This short section describes best practice that will ensure that you get great results.

Cleaning the Eggs

1 I wash my eggs in warm water (at room temperature so that the contents of the egg don't cook). I then pat them and lay them out on a tea towel or other absorbent surface to let them dry off completely.

2 After I have blown out the contents (see page 122), I give the egg another wash, holding it under a stream of water and letting the water run inside the hole. I give the egg a gentle shake to allow the water to clean out the inside, then blow out the water and let the egg dry as before.

How to Hold an Egg

Eggs are fairly sturdy, but can break quite easily if dropped. To avoid dropping and breaking the egg, I rest it on a paper towel on my work surface while I'm working on it. I have seen people holding the egg in mid-air; however, this is not feasible for hours at a time.

How to Blow Out an Egg

The traditional way of blowing out an egg is to make two holes, one at each end, and then to blow out the contents.

1 Poke a small hole in the top of the egg with a drawing pin. Gently press the pointy end into the egg, twisting it carefully once it's through the shell to widen the hole. You could also use any object that has a thin, pointed tip, such as a needle or a tiny screwdriver.

2 Flip the egg over and poke a slightly larger hole in the bottom. This is the hole the yolk and white will come out of.

3 Insert your pointed tool into either hole and wiggle it around to break up the yolk, so that it blows out more easily. It is advisable to do this over a bowl in case any of the contents of the egg leak out.

4 Hold the egg over a bowl to catch the yolk and white, then blow through the small hole at the top. The contents of the egg should come out of the bottom hole as you blow.

5 Once the contents have been removed, hold the egg with the top hole facing up under running water so that it runs through the egg and out of the bottom hole, thus rinsing out the inside of the egg.

TIP

SET THE EGG ON A TEA TOWEL OR OTHER ABSORBENT SURFACE TO DRY OFF. ENSURE THE EGG IS COMPLETELY DRY BEFORE PAINTING OR DYEING, OTHERWISE THE COLOURS MAY RUN OR WIPE OFF.

Using a Stylus

Before you begin drawing the design, you need to choose the right stylus for the job. Styluses come in many sizes, but I have used a small, medium and large for the projects in this book. Use a small stylus for fine, delicate lines; a large stylus for filling in large sections; and a medium stylus for everything else.

1 Heat the head of the stylus over the flame of a candle for 10 seconds.

2 Scoop a small amount of beeswax into the funnel of the stylus. If you are using honeycomb wax, rip it into small strips and feed it through the top of the stylus, being careful not to touch the hot stylus head.

3 Reheat the stylus over the candle flame until the beeswax has melted. Don't leave the stylus over the flame for too long, otherwise the beeswax will get too warm and 'blob' when you try to create your pattern. Holding the stylus over the flame for a count of three should be sufficient.

4 Test the flow of the beeswax from the stylus on a piece of scrap paper before you start drawing on your egg. You can either draw the pattern with a pencil first, and follow the guidelines with the stylus and beeswax, or draw directly onto the egg with your stylus and beeswax.

Filling the Hole Before Dyeing

Closing off the hole at the bottom of the egg will prevent the dye from flooding the egg.

1 Pinch off a bit of warm beeswax with your fingernails and roll it into a cone shape.

2 Insert this beeswax plug into the hole at the bottom of the egg and squash it down a bit.

3 Fill a stylus with beeswax and draw a line of wax around the base of the plug, where it meets the sides of the hole, to seal it.

Removing the Wax Plug After Dyeing

Before melting the beeswax pattern off the entire egg, it is important to remove the wax plug first, so the egg does not explode.

1 Heat a pointed tool, such as a drawing pin or a needle, over a candle flame.

2 Insert the pointed tool into the plug, melting it open.

TIP

YOU CAN ALSO USE THE TIP OF A KNIFE OR YOUR FINGERNAIL TO LIFT OFF THE WAX SEAL.

Dyeing the Egg

Throughout the book, I have used aniline dyes that require a teaspoon of vinegar to activate the pigment. However, you can use food colourings available at your local store instead.

1 Place the egg in the dye solution and spin it around until it is coated.

2 Gently push the egg down into the solution with a cup, so it is fully submerged in the dye.

3 Submerge the egg for 10–20 minutes until it reaches the desired colour. It's important to turn the egg part way through the process to avoid uneven dyeing and light spots where it touches the container. Remove the egg from the dye and blot it dry with a paper towel.

Removing Wax from the Entire Egg

This is my favourite part of the egg-art process – when the wax is removed and the patterns are revealed.

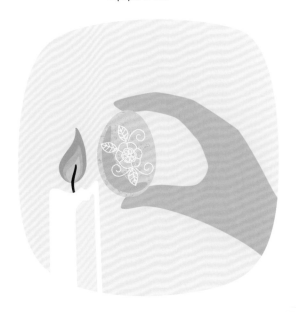

1 Starting at the bottom of the egg and working your way up, hold the egg next to (but not in) the candle flame to avoid burn marks.

2 As the beeswax melts, wipe it off with a tissue. If there are stubborn areas of beeswax, use a craft knife to scrape them off.

INDEX

CREDITS

I would like to thank the team at Quarto for making this book possible, for reaching out to me, for trusting me to photograph every step and for working on each egg design to make it fun and easy for you to follow.

I am thankful for my family; for my daughter, who sits by me and watches me work, and for my husband, who speaks so proudly about what I do. He says I am an artist, a rock star and that I make incredible eggs. I am not a rock star – just a very well-skilled batik artist and painter. I like to stay humble and true to my art style. Trends come and go, patterns evolve, dyes improve – but the old art of batik eggs stays the same.

Finally, thanks to you, my readers, who think the projects in this book are worth a try. Enjoy it and don't limit yourself to the egg art shown here – get creative, go further and try to invent your own designs.